D0707579

PARISH KREWES

PARISH KREWES

MICAH BALLARD

BOOTSTRAP PRESS
LOWELL, MA

© Copyright, the right to copy down words, was instituted under Henry VIII.

First published in 2009

Bootstrap Productions
82 Wyman Street
Lowell, MA 01852

Bootstrap Press is an imprint of Bootstrap Productions, Inc., a non-profit arts and literary collective founded by Derek Fenner and Ryan Gallagher.

Cover Art by David Meltzer.
Author photograph by Sunnylyn Thibodeaux.

ISBN 978-0-9821600-1-5

Some of these poems first appeared in the following: Le Palais de Nuit, Morning Train, Blue Book #8, Damn the Caesars III, Blue Press Portfolio, Greetings #11: A Magazine of the Sound Arts, Pax Americana, Slow Parade, Derivations, Dirty Swamp Poets, Big Bell #2, NCOC Review, Eoagh #3: Queering Language, kadar koli, Big Bridge #10: "An Open Letter to America," and Big Bridge #11: "Tribute to David Meltzer"; the anthologies: Evidence of the Paranormal (Owl Press, 2003) and Bay Poetics (Faux Press, 2005); and books: Bettina Coffin (Red Ant, 2003), Emblematic (Old Gold, 2004), Unforeseen (Fauxpress/e, 2004), Wrought Iron & Burgundy (Auguste, 2005), Evangeline Downs (Ugly Duckling Presse, 2006), and Darrell (Blue Press, 2007).

This publication was made possible by donations to Bootstrap Productions, Inc. Please visit our online catalogue and consider helping us support contemporary arts and literary culture.

Bootstrap Productions
www.bootstrapproductions.org
Distributed to the trade by Small Press Distribution.

THIS IS A BOOTSTRAP PRODUCTION!

CONTENTS

INVITATION

The guests have left
voices from
the old palace

gone. We hold
their hymns

written in revenge
& give entrance
to those

      who follow.

COMMUNIQUÉ

How faded
        without others
        Congo Square

under diluvial night sky.
How far
        since we slept
        these steps
        before waking alone?

I see them there
        here, no shirt
        hair over eyes
        leaned back
against that stone wall
which finds mine
as I lead you

"We are between time"
 as the old Cajuns would say

Not on sides
ambivalent to none
our roads
        shortened
        born past
before leaving

But those evenings have gone
turned back

to unchartered
worlds

outbound stations
new words

        that figure no map

from Poydras to Kenner

from Violet to Metairie

from Meraux to Bucktown

from Village de L'Est to Old Metairie

from Chalmette to Lakeview

from Arabi to Mid-City

from Lower Ninth to Broadmoor

from New Orleans East to Gentilly

from Bywater to Treme

MONDAY

The silence
is not permanent

old walls
where no nail can penetrate

& books from the 17th
century housed
below.

There must
be somewhere else

to kill, someone
other to usher
in the new

all the wires
now down, connections lost.

EAST ANNEX

A dull boom
       inside the tube
       pale flashes
                then ten minutes
for the whole dormitory

High Mass

& a low sloping vault
curved at its peak.

Asleep in the earth
small bones
         divide into beds,
         parallel ribs

& a little bronze snake melted down
where the bullet went thru.

Pale flashes
      a drop of ink to penetrate the cracks

long waits, short drags
weeded spheres
to loosen the outline

darker ink
& a crease in the paper

short
drags   long waits,

ATONEMENT

Along alleyways
they wait

for us to be alone.
We roll deep
& dive out

with our wants.
We choose
to chase another

tone home, it is
vast & seeks also

foreign bellows.

QUARANTINE

Alone
in their keeping

small doses

endeavor to induce a pastime.
Cut
to carry us closer

we take them by day
& lie

on the floor

to return once more.

MAGNOLIA

Late winter. We trip
in & out of each other's
morning. The sky lingers
in folds of blue then
red. Far off the streets
wind & band around
the mountains. Our eyes
are shot with smoke.
There is no more water left.
The last ferry has met
where the sun will set,
a single dove lands on
the windowsill. We pour
ourselves a glass of sherry
& lay down under what
becomes the moon.

POEM

Dark
as the hands

that hold us
we just lay here

with
our waiting & wants
as the war

drags on to yet unknown

        riding out
        against.

E.ST.V.M.

From this hour
my hand a silver cask

cool with pearl
these alcoves

plus newfound grief
matter not. By now

the moon shall wane
the Olympian god cracked

in two, this too shall pass
this muting of the mind

a diamond's dust
cruel at best.

ODE TO WILL YACKULIC

Fortified by the hand of modern mediums
almost all his pyramids contain the remains
of our two largest legacies. Undergoing

many transformations he stands over our tattoos
& cares not for ridicule. Crushed over bones
let there be no headstones, for only these

preliminaries serve to prepare our consecration.
Despite other tries this one died just once
& the later twice. "The light that loses, the night

that wins." Before then he would place their
ashes into three pendulums, the first of which
could render its wearer invisible. Now, fated

as the most skilled dissector of his time
we prefer the others to be swallowed, used only
for channeling & taken out the mouth like this.

SOLSTICE

Gone now this evening
his scent over afternoon
brandy. Early dinner
without friend or family
walking far enough
to catch a ride back,
it's better to keep moving
the longing no longer easy
suspicion less likely. But
we shall forget he came
here tonight & will remember,
waiting at the window
watching the wake go by.

PUTREFACTION

for Patrick Dunagan

Of morning
& by tomorrow midday
many will vow to
begin the celebration
anyway. Dug out
or covered by cloth
gold from the hands
& feet are taken off.
Bearing the dates
& epitaphs between
they turn from outer
to inner & care not
whose spell they cast.
Found to bring direct curses
their molds are worn
atop the teeth
& are said to be inscribed
v.s.o.p. Pointing to
their ruins, lamentations
like this one need no
introduction.

Royal Aces
Crescent City Claver
Les Femmes Enchantress
Westside Revealers
Toast of the Vikings
Original Four Roses
Nile Queen
Krewe of Ramses Inc.
Krewe of Nefertiti
Gardenia Stitch & Chat Club
El Diablos
Gay Twenties
Society of Social Celebrities
Stand Together Club
Cuban Queens Carnival
Zulu Social Aid & Pleasure

DIABOLIQUE

Or at dawn
when the purse folds open

& over the sink
queens weep
with ashes

of ivory sorrow
the solstice
of a phantom cry

lies beyond the palace
of another world

& still the dust drips
from hardened lips
by way of vanity

& namesake
to cultivate fate

in the mouths of the living

BENEDICTION

They should like
to be quiet, motionless
no more alive than
before. But now the

royal ghosts are calling
the empty theatres
their thieves, harlots their
garlands. Is it the toil

in spirit or sounds
of open tombs that after
time one becomes numb
& so the hour no longer

comes. Last night
her body was carried
to a small wagon
& a death mask—

cast of her face
& hands was made.
Gone are the guests
bones of those who

have not stood alone.
Buried early morning
& involuntary exile
may their remains

cease to be released
& her name left behind
as both signature
& sign.

9/13/96

Nefertiti over
right pec & serpent
with jaws open
on left shoulder.
German cross

with Exodus 18:11
across back, Playaz
on nape of neck.
Christ in crown
of thorns & flames

on left biceps
Heartless with skull
& crossbones on right.
50 Niggaz over sternum
FTW in script

across shoulder
blades & trapazoids.
Laugh Now with mask
of Comedy on lower
sides of back, Cry

Later with mask
of Tragedy. Outlaw
down left forearm
Thug Life with bullet
across abs.

NIGHT PRAYER

Bring to his bed
company, so that
he might rest again.
Lay them down
one after another

& let them leave
or enter all as to
their own coming
or going. See
that his beard be

trimmed, tab paid
& poems printed.
Bring to his lips
a kiss & heart
a similar start,

the words to deny
what others want
& chance to change
what forgotten's
past. See to him

that opportunity's
granted beyond repair
& that he use it well
further than its telling.
Bring to his life

a life after death
& one that's as
inwardly kept
as he is open
to all outside.

MADRIGAL

Seems
a whole decade's

passed
since last we lived him.
                Strange
he used to pretend
to be released

but there were others
who wished him
                    dead.

Now
it's almost as if
he alone

must have known
showing up   so vividly
in our

never collected.

EN ROUTE

for Jeff Butler

Scores of letters, telegrams & poems
Lie unread on the table. Veiled in the folds
Neglected light, there are no more arches
Only wall & shadow. Head of Nero
Bone-pin & scissor, in uniform departure
They pass in procession & do not stand up
To cold or hunger. We keep moving, making
A white cross over both wrist & shoulder.
This does not work well. There are five marks
The first of which enables life after death
So let the first override the third & second
Override the fourth. There are no
Excavations here, only private vaults
Ceremonies left without safe keeping.

FORTHCOMING

The first hours
past each searchlight
        you live
out your past life
            in exchange for a first

a series of etchings
to petrify the lines

one watches the entrance
while another turns the bed

an iron
headrest

a dull blade to clean

infinite odes scraped to dust

only a powdering
then back thru the wall

hollow chambers
      a new map
          to burn

LITURGY

Far from hotel, city street & travel
we return not harmed
but rather come back to scenes
already dreamed.
Given our final votive offering
she is it, Black Amber with Pole Star.
Inverted & hung over chest
let there be no regret
For without it living does not forgive
nor relation rank pure to those
already born. Without revenge
might they be carried across
& faces from the street turn back
to those passed in a crowded barroom.
Oh it all gets lost, "that's how
reflection & retaliation becomes
not bound." Hidden from within,
may we serve to interpret the signs
& as a shore to our wanderings
become one with the vast silence
which moves manifold
to their design.

INITIATION

Stretch out the skin
& ink each
limb as other men.

Do not think
of the past

it has long since
vanished.
& why with tomorrow

its secrets
lie with strangers.
If love

is an only way
to admit

then let us rise
to walk its ruins,
the lure

of a distant port
the poem to its course.

SLUMP GRIND

A cut on top the hand
& blood smeared slightly below left eye
This morning last night, yesterday
jumped without shadow only sound
a second time not this one but
last I arrived with headphones, his
a pair of Gucci glasses. Defeat has always
been denied me. Unless created out
of my own design, a con for the senses.
The mirrors behind do not lie. His face
haunts not but remains a dark hood
hooded with only whites of eyes & teeth
running uphill while ready we watch
with broken glass under arm, aluminum
bat echoing off cement.

BAYOU ST. JOHN

Held for murder one
    he wore a slight build
        short hair
fixed to a crown.
Brought down
    to enter the earth
    the parlor prayers
are said
societies benevolent to the beauty
within each.
    But we get lost
        stagger to talk
  always the unattainable
  always the irreproachable

    libations of spirit
        where all turns contrast
Lend us able
    pharmacies
    to still the messengers
        keep quiet
these lives that are not our own
but are given

    as he to the ground
    lost as we are
        to the passing
          the sounding

FOR TOOKIE

Chamber to chamber
all the slabs
        crack

& to trace the years
between

his body rose to become younger.
Stretched out before us

we find the way
for written in walls

his words weigh all
& they are to be heard

by many.

ANONYMOUS

Shots ring out
& cut in the night rain
strands of matted hair
with white enamel
do their work
in the hour of Mars.
Bowing before them
"it is only the maiden trying to get in"
& this is her story silent.
Here for the undertaking
what matter the body & its scars,
wars thru which it has passed.
Set in sapphire
& strung about the neck
there is no breath left
Carved upon the rock
the catacombs are locked
& time will not vanquish
these letters.

Easy Life Powder	$ .50
Love Powder	.25
Sacred Sand	1.00
Black Cat Oil	1.00
Goofer Dust	.50
Dragon's Blood	2.50
Boss-Fix Powder	.25
Controlling Oil	.50
Get Together Drops	1.00

with Cedar Sigo

EX VOTO

Make us
what given we are to become,

reveal to us
what fortunes

lost of this city
there are left to borrow.

Keep them close
as these things that sing next to us

who are not here

but reside like breaths alongside the neck.

ADDENDUM

Arm in arm
then used to adorn
each statue

graphs of the colonnade
close the gateway

& seated in his phantom
the chorus is changed,
chant rearranged.

Taking the stake
& chain with them

clans of this kind
do not remove the mind
but learn to take refuge

in opium then wine.
Capable of many,

not a trace of them remains
just the reclaiming
of lives

that have never lived here
that have only themselves to warn.

CONTINUUM

With sovereign ease
he uncovered each cloth
to bring forth the offerings.
Ring of St. Elizabeth

Ring of St. Valentine
open to the chant
days have gone by yet
the hour is no longer

alive. What have we done
to dismiss it? The robes
are laid out, beds set
veils brought down.

Ordered underground
& still to be found
let no one enter
this room, no thing

be left behind to find.
Without escort
& seen only in dreams
might these bones

regain again their flesh
& this caveau stay closed
open only for the living
who we take from rest.

MANDALA

Given
are the newly
those risen from rest
swamps off the same

shoreline. Miles out
from the moss & trees
they arrive in dream
& lay around by day

to come to a better
understanding. Out
from envelopes in oaks
their fire burns low

& they hear us slam
& carry. It would be
better for us to leave
until we know what

we are doing.
Holding our breath
from the other side
they let us pass by

for we too illustrate
eternal & emptied
of our flasks
lie with the unspoken.

ENVOI

Necropolis seal
                over entrance passage
        in terminal caps
                covered by a linen pall

        The effigy of which
                is slid to staples
                        lest they be
                                under eaves

                                to enter the earth
                the Sherry
                        Netherlands
                                dagger & sheath

                        with the minarets
                        of Metairie
                                beneath.

FLAMBEAU

There are two red chambers
& you are on the other side
only ashes. The vines along

the wall tell all, but what
remains? Old habits return
nightlife wanes & ordained

to find the source we scan
the sky for her war-torch.
Children of the Dead, House

of Napoleon, cobra & carnelian
where do the dawns draw out?
Far off & legendary

may the voices recall their lives
the brides remain lost to hide
for there is no age here

just these walls of ivy
with single trumpets
of blood.

UNFORESEEN

It would be evening
& no longer marked by the design
of wings
who lay outstretched before
that by war
& love of it alike
we continue to watch time
recalling first
the reflection transcribed at our sides.
But martyred world
which waits to break in live tragedy
gaunt with secrets
we need no more
so relight the embers
that we may find ourselves with the night
for uncertain to none
the descent has begun
& there is no turning back
only moving forth
without returning.

FIRST CONJURE

Come
bring all there is to be had

Leave
the rest, take them to their places

Live
not their deaths but raise them all

Speak
through the one as with the other

Wait, listen, & call.

MORNING TRAIN

It is a simple court, the use's song
however difficult the phrasing moves along
or is it the burden of living without
skating or walking to work
pretending there's no pretense of neglect
as recognition for weekly temperament
Already the body tired from waking
already the shadow of chandelier
across ceiling or legs of sofa stretched over floor
reminds one of how it all began
that there is more time to mend the mind
& make one's mark no matter the progress
Yet always have I found myself in others
their lineage remained
however vacant or ill-fitted. It is an
inner coding, doors of the same shrine
galleys to fill the next void. Or saying goodbye
knowing you'll never meet again
but will hear one another
in the turning of pages or typing of letters
from one state to another.

BORROWED TIME
for Kevin Opstedal

Not a book
    left to sell
    not a bottle
of wine to spill.
    Not a cigarette
              to smoke
              not a bag of herbs to toke
    Not a woman
        to ease the mind
              nor an alley
              to find one's kind.
Not a poem left to sing
              drawing framed
       to bring
       not a friend to offend
              stranger
              to welcome again.
        Not a city I'd rather be
         or ocean hidden
                  to see
              not a place to lie the head
              Else a room
              to rent instead.

LUNDI GRAS / 5PM

Sleeping
back of trolley
waiting
for the next stop
or response
from a call never sent

It's all recompense
these days
ways in which we implore,
ignore one another

Those who left
leave to stay
their own terms
own grievances
false things,
deceased

In their telling
alive in their keeping
& everyone else who goes
            (also knows)
as we all do
coming back the same
condemning one another

as we have
like we want not to.

BLED WHITE

Quick
to rage with them
these worlds, their war
tears on the canvas.
Half our lives
torn together.
Quick to rage without them
to rage within their empty spaces
to hold each battle inside
blood on the walls
I take from their mouths.
We initiate one another
I am in front. In the night
They are in front when
we sit down to bleed
We face one another in the dark.

VIEUX CARRÉ

In these vaults
the blades are bright
darker love

is demanded.
May it be shot

or shadow
there is only fear

of empty years
as light falls

green on the table.

Napoleon House
500 Chartres St.
New Orleans, La.

November 25, 2005

TO THE 9TH WARD

The parishes
are gone
no sound now
        to drown away
        the sighs

Bodies rise
in the dark of morning
& hot winds

pervade
        the balustrades

Thick debris
settles over

while mold dampens the walls.

A small boat
        approaches the roof

& we just sit here
waiting in ruin

with nothing
particular to say.

INTERIM

Maybe
some day you'll see me
in the country
          or parish swamps

outside City Hall
riding up escalator
past the parades
of yesteryear

lamplit
bombing the hill
under morning sun
& I'll come back

          blonde & tan
the long winded loneliness
gone, debris thin
air thick

& neither seen nor known
open this book
which was bound for you

          with or without
          my being here.

NEW MOON

What more
    is there, something
    else other
        than this?
        There is no further
this is it
no current now to wash away
the signs
already the image   emptied
           shifted sands
                laid to channels.
But to ride out again
as of old
      "with a longing like your own"
     as in that secret noon

where the compulsions
wear out & each one
        is left behind
        to fade as they may

so might we tonight
      leaving no trace
      or better, just one
to be left as evidence
however
close

or far off   the encounter

QUEENS TUNNEL TO LEXINGTON

Not enough
sleep
dreams where the real
life is lived
Surrendered realms
which initiate
the inner workings of deals
left undone.
Until there are none to be done.
Only
the premonition
of where we'll be when they arrive
& what's next
after they're gone.
It all returns. But is it morning
or am I still here from yesterday?
Blood rushes below. Rain
seeps through windowpanes
the bell
rings. Stop. I will not rise
to receive their grievances
nor their praise, false ambitions
material poetry.
There is another communion to tune in with
Something more immediate than flesh.

TO THE BOGS AT TOLLUND & GRAUBALLE

This is the last
of the jewelry box
gone dry & on his head
he wore a pointed

skin cap, "a life for
a life," both the dead
& sleeping. Instead
of thread, iron rings

a succession
of sharp cuts could be
seen down his back.
Keep them fixed

at the temples
they do not stamp
his gentleness as
the following tears.

After drying out
he measured only
five feet ten inches
& both his hands

& feet appeared
to have been bound.
Locks from the fore-
head & neck gather

downward, only braids
& quantities of fair hair
survive. The arrangement
of which remains

human ash & resin
on metal. Preserved
for centuries
may this blood

initiate their rites
& these bones
serve as both ritual,
sacrifice.

NOVEMBER COMING

Hallowed out, the branchings
bleed away

two hearts passed
to the altar

It is the crowded
home of ghosts,
gathering of song

        dark woods beating
        at the window.

ALL SAINTS DAY

for Sunnylyn

There are sobs in the distance
twin forces among the pines
           steps lead further
                    voices return
                    & under eyes of idols
                    the influence is united.
Dashed off first as rough drafts
these are the only scripts that survive
                our cemetery years.

Despite further attention to detail
they do not record our failure of removal
or methods of disposal.
                 Since then we've been divided
                 & the theme of death is our theifhood.

Pressed into flesh like this   the sickness of pearl
has been a remedy for centuries
              indicating years spent in imprisonment

Some are referred to as Suites of Diamonds
              others Hearts,
              according to custom

              finds of this kind have no contradiction
              & are said to be worn at the temples
                    summoned to dwell within

They stand alone in their eternity
& are not able to give

                    direct orders.

SELAH

Or
to lay back
the head

& hear their hymns
as already
said

an endless trip
without stress of confidence

hands
rising up

beneath.

EVOCATION

From the grounds
of Old Metairie
& hallways thru pyramids

with unnumbered bones
to the 3 St. Louises
& live oaks of Cypress Grove

onward we carry
whatever has traced our
way. So might the soil

turn over– Apparitions
come forth, this path
hath only one following

one way to get away.
East of these walls
& never to be returned

let it be said
the oath has been told
sold for the taking. Not

again will these vaults
faces hide, never
to end their dens

which do not stop
but drop to that final place
where all is erased.

NOLA

Walled between sides
        & combed for gold then weapons
        impossible in hours
we take on
their looks. Now it is our turn

        to go among the masked
        past balconies
of St. Charles & Decatur
                down boulevards
         thru tunnels that lead to the gulf.
         Yet in these domes
where roam ghosts of yesteryear
interesting how our litanies
are still to be welcomed
        how arranged to fall
        the loss thereof
             unites all.
Woe to him
whose crimes block the way
woe to him whose levee
takes away
        Placed upon the pedestal
        & held in cells for weeks,

evacuation has yet to be ritual
Only some are left to sleep.

Hurricane Katrina

ATCHAFALAYA

Drowned down
they awaken not
but
    ascend

to join in
with the earth inside them.

Parallel
       to the passing

"might we hasten to arise"

& gather their sands
        for other demands.

PAPER LANTERN

Thru narrow towers
inside a green light
which molds the shadow where we stand
false portrait
of life
whose faces outnumber
who is it this time
will hold
the lantern? There is nothing left
yet a name, no one here
save a voice from beyond
& if to go on
past the draperies of Canal,
down Bourbon
where the dance still lingers
back to Burgundy
with these waters
that might never drain away
what will arrive to relieve
our stay? When gone
from the scene of everything,
it is she
who keeps this alive
as with her various company
no threshold is denied.

NEW RITES

Each bears
the same name
having turned white from night.

Strange
they should call back

apparitions

who've left no trace,
whose fate has followed

& passed into present.
Crowned inferior
& assigned

to the ascendancy
might each life

sufficed
show within their wounds
& if something inside

speak different

then to it also are we a medium
an open chant for all.

PORT OF CALL

It must be a question of endurance
a confirmation never to conform
to remain variable as at a distance
finally done with the day, done
before the voices stop so bodies
drop over stones we walk upon.
What then when we get there,
a stolen Charles d'Orleans book
or shovel for another biography?
There is no one else to acknowledge it.
They are gone to this world & it is
ours through which they speak.
We have seen them since birth
& only now half-heard their call.

BOOK OF ESTHER

From obscurity
rises the unknown
   neither father nor mother
Ishtar or Hadassah

to quarters
are the young sent
   To citadels
   the heritage hidden
   decree set

"For you asked of nothing"
 obtained favor from all

were purified
as with oil & myrrh
   custodial orders

as scepter & crown
or signet ring
post gallows,

while whole tribes
   were hanged
   in his name
& on the 14th day
Purim, or pur
   a lot cast against
   a new feast
deliverance.

INHERITANCE

Always
this elation

shaped
from a space

       beyond

an alien
presence

ordered to dictate

a guest
of flesh

where new light
       penetrates.

NOCTURNE

From the flickering in this room
To footsteps that fade every other second
Back towards words which droop to the ground
spelt backwards starting from sound.

We turn our backs to the cheerful scene,
The blood of another woman
boiling thru the veins.
Interlaced by laughs of a lesser frequency

these knives have become
Our mirror. Underneath their blades
there is one scar who tells everything.
& it disappears into a wound

of a foreign design
somewhat like this cigarette
I throw from the window
that forms a pentagram
As it flies by.

ZEITGEIST

Without food
or forty
we make it uphill
back from the bar
where we were
much stronger.

Now the face
has gone afraid
the body burns
head throbs. We
have not slept
for weeks

yet the hours
get shorter, poems
go unfinished.
Burnt out our songs
are sung & the high-
way follows slow

behind. But who
are the next ones
who will hold
their own, back
downhill at the bar
without food
or forty.

CELLAR FURROWS

A cold rue to the forefront
two hundreds & a butterfly knife
to cop another castle keep
the first hours wind, then infinite silence
minute swamps black to their centers
the light that passes thru
a simple white gift dusted into lines
live embers off chimney sweeps
you are there you are above
you are there above, a suitcase
at the station, chain & crosspiece
open airways to comb the smoke
crimp the lashes, "a life on the tracks"
blind alleys seen in the next.

INTERLUDE

Enough
to be back on the scene
lost

in chemical weavings
these fogged
                    hollows

we dive.
Where else can we go,
gone as we already are

contained by a world
no war
will satisfy

& how long
does it take to endure

divided

as we are
further than years before,
closer

without the company

AN OPEN LETTER

Having no past
        but present
It would be easy
            to keep going
    having others do to others
                    what one wills of them
                never willing oneself.

To want so much
        to be   inside
                    as if gifts could provide
        that like semblance
            absent in each hour.

                    But he directs
            the unmoving
                    moved as they are

                            against.
    It would be easy
    all that credit
        charmed as labor
                    but we will not labor
                    for what's lost

                        taken by his own pride
            off another's
                            tongue.

    I see it as my own

have taken it as my own
        wore it as a badge
                a shadow in a face
        we can no longer name
                no longer call upon
however
        unwanted or asked.

If you had asked, no

    if you had
            wanted to.

        We shall step away

        gather what we know
        as attack,
                that force within
    that began with or without
                        them
"To keep one's friends close
            enemies closer"

            To be both

            The young we were (are)
    watches without fear
        welcomes it
                as we are born into
        & will carry out alone
                regardless
                        the solitude.

The unspoken is enough.

The worlds within
                  worlds of their own
                  Uninhabited.

            Long is the way
                for those who intercede
                        between

        "Send the Guards back to their Kind"

           a trick played on time

                phantom of the mind

ESPLANADE

Unpaid
& faded ashore
      facing South

    the morrow's morning.

          Black curls
          night tides

relax the muscles
      solace to loan
         a last breath

    gulf winds caught

          from
          tributary years

RUE TOULOUSE

For decades we lived thru them
Baton Rouge, Maurice, River Ridge
but the world was a yard of statues
& each one resembled her face. Those
who imprisoned watched the guards
as earthed inside, seasoned to provide
love from another divinity. We lived
thru them & are survived by none.
But already they've come, the months
& years, new solitudes fired up later
then left to stay. Put them all away.
Blot out name & face until the next
ones come to herald the way, wade off
the waters & take what's left

THE MOORS & GLENS

Steal a hanker
chief

and pin it down to a toad

beneath
the water   of a stream.

         Each pin
           marking the name
of the enemy
As the cloth wastes

              away
       So will the body

            of her
            his who had worn it.

BUTTE LA ROSE

Lifted from within

    each wreath flowers round
    & to raise their beds

        lapis lazuli
        with shell inlay
        hold the back

    in a coating of wax.
    Stuffed from the same
            substance,

        we too went South
        before hardening

    & taking its soil with us
    seep also
           gray vapors.

PSALM

Most burnt
the evening lung of our love
from it we carry an urn
of brightest ember

Winds lift it up
as the quarter moon
in our vision of Congo Square.

It wears a white gown
& whispers loudly
it flees as we do
gaining entrance to hearts
& remembers
a creole song about loss

written in winter
to couplets by morning

Afloat
are those ashes

caught in the furnace
of feeling. We too wade further
now older than they

younger still than thou.
Or how they really do
build back
sing the same song

as those past before.
They are dark
& live with us

    we have light, behind them we lead.

DARRELL

Too late
　　　　to be giving this
　　　　　　passing by to say hello
　　　　　　　　& bum a smoke
　　　even tho I don't anymore.

　　　　　　　All the pills, stationary
　　　　　　　　　or Sauvignon Blanc
　　　　　　we shared as
　　　　　　　　　　trade for conversation
　　　　　for something to say
　　　　　　　　　　as if there was something.

　　You greeted us
　　　　　our first apartment
　　　　　　led us
　　　　　　into a life to lead
　　　　　　　　however different we were
　　　　　　　　　difficult we are

　　　　　　from one another.
　　I see you, alone
　　　　　　waiting for the next meal
　　　　　　rearranging the little furniture

　　　　　　you had left
　　　　　　　　after giving it all away
　　as you always did
　　　　just to reorder
　　　　　the same thing,

87

or talking on the phone

to an old friend
asking for company
at your convenience
as I tried today
hearing that you're gone.

I don't believe them
him who on the bus
this morning
said

they found you two months ago.

We passed you later/sooner than that
& I have here your hat
a new one from New Orleans
almost like the one
we gave you
less than a year ago.

I hear you there
rather me here
Sunnylyn banging

on your door
& later crying outside
while I crawled on the floor
trying

to save my books
& poems

from the fire
cracking at those windows.
Today is Sunday
& I figured I'd see you
outside the Orbit Room
shaved head & earring

beard slightly grown in
& cane propped
against stool.

You had that look
as if all was nigh
or had been
since you moved on
from that
past life.
You said "there were no regrets"
& there shouldn't be
with everything, every day
& said that
every time
you knocked
palms full of pills, new stationary
copies of letters
to the building manager

or your laminated business card
silver letters pressed

over black.

I'm glad that you got
   to speak with your aunt
   finally, come to terms
     with distance of family

  Glad that you tried to break
    into our apartment
     (on accident) on speed
      or would open that window

    from your bathroom
    to hand me a smoke
     when I was

  graphing the walls with Butcher paper

You laughed at that
 laughed at me
   when I showed up a year later
    after moving to Fillmore
     & walked down that beautiful hall,

lobby which we once shared.

   Asked what I took
     because I shook too much
   then pulled
    those pictures

      of Sunnylyn & I
      YOU & HER

       & our first books
             which we signed, unwillingly.

I see them there, on your shelf
           next to the champagne glasses

            you never drank out of
            across the wall
            all the pictures taken
                  down

          now framed blank
             from nicotine stains

          with new ones inside each.
I see that one of you & I inside

         your hair cut & dyed
           mine longer, mustache thicker

           & I wonder
            was it still there
               as you lay on your cot
with window half-
            way open
            was anyone there
               or had been

        as you sat alone, finished your smoke

          & looked up

exhaling one last time

as often you did
as often we will

Always be thankful

of You.

VALEDICTION

At last
induced to some hallowed order
for the sinister songs
relied upon
have been abandoned.
From the soundless shadows
light itself brings
there are no words but thought
no sounds
but feeling. Yet when the poem
comes undone
we do nothing but turn away.
Oh life lavish & playing its parts!
with no farewells
or private partings
just untimely avarice designed from afar
where tomorrow ceases to exist
& today remains an open door
an only entrance
into its abyss.

Micah Ballard was born in Baton Rouge, Louisiana in 1975. He attended the University of Southwestern Louisiana and the Poetics program at New College of California, where from 2000-7 he directed the Humanities program. With Sunnylyn Thibodeaux, he is co-editor for Auguste Press and currently works for the MFA in Writing program at the University of San Francisco.